ERIC HU

Oh No They **AREN'T**

NATURE

What are you waiting for? Turn the page and dive right in!

ILLUSTRATED BY
SAM CALDWELL

words & pictures

© 2025 Quarto Publishing Group USA Inc.
Text © Eric Huang 2025
Illustrations © Sam Caldwell 2025

First published in 2025 by words & pictures,
an imprint of The Quarto Group.
100 Cummings Center,
Suite 265D Beverly,
MA 01915, USA.
T (978) 282-9590 F (978) 283-2742
www.quarto.com

Copyeditor: Nancy Dickmann
Project Editor: Alice Hobbs
Designer: Kathryn Davies
Production Manager: Nikki Ingram
Creative Director: Malena Stojić
Associate Publisher: Holly Willsher

A CIP record for this book is available from the Library of Congress.

ISBN: 978-0-7112-9277-2

Manufactured in Guangdong, China TT102024

9 8 7 6 5 4 3 2 1

ERIC HUANG

Oh No They AREN'T
NATURE

FASCINATING FACTS YOU NEVER KNEW ABOUT THE NATURAL WORLD!

ILLUSTRATED BY
SAM CALDWELL

words&pictures

CONTENTS

INTRODUCTION......................................**6**

PREHISTORIC LIFE.........................**8**
The First Creatures
Ancient Seas
Age of Reptiles
Age of Mammals

GREEN PLANET............................**16**
The Air We Breathe
Leafy Giants
Five a Day
Flower Power
Fun Guys

UNDER THE SEA...........................**26**
Surf and Turf
Marine Metropolis
Oceanic Orchestra
Swimming the Seven Seas

Slow down and uncover nature's secrets.

Get caught
in a web of
fascinating facts.

CREEPY-CRAWLIES................................34
World Wide Web
Social Butterflies
Slime Time
Pulling Your Leg

PREDATOR AND PREY........................42
Catch me if you Can
Shark Attack
Hide and Seek
Smell you Later

HIGH FLIERS.................................50
Going with the Flow
High Rolling
Aerial Acrobatics
Grounded

GEOLOGICAL TIMELINE....................58
GLOSSARY.....................................60
ABOUT THE AUTHOR AND ILLUSTRATOR......64

This book
puts the FUN
in fungus!

INTRODUCTION

The world around us is full of life—and not just in nature reserves and national parks. There are plants, animals, and all kinds of living things right in your town or city. They live in your backyard, in your house, and even *inside you!*

Many of us take care of potted plants and share our homes with pets, while some people are lucky to live in a jungle or forest or next to a body of water where a wide variety of animals and plants also live.

No matter where you call home, nature is there. You just have to look for it. **But how much do you really know about nature?**

We all know that prehistoric animals like dinosaurs roamed Earth before humans were around. They're all extinct. . . aren't they?

And everyone knows that plants, unlike animals, get all the energy they need from sunlight instead of food. . . right?

And we're familiar with animals like camels that have water-filled humps to survive desert journeys, penguins that are all cold-weather birds, and little lemmings that are rodents that run off the edges of cliffs. . . aren't we?

OH NO THEY AREN'T!

In fact, quite a lot of what you think you know about all creatures great and small turns out to be false!

READ ON to encounter **critters** so small you'll need a microscope to see them, living things that inhabited our planet millions and millions of years before people, and familiar organisms from **whales and cows** to **vegetables and fruits**, **birds and bugs** to **flowers and mushrooms**.

NATURE AHEAD

PREHISTORIC LIFE
THE FIRST CREATURES

Life first appeared on Earth about 3.8 billion years ago, but it didn't look like you or me. Humans are made of trillions of cells, but the first living organisms had just one cell each. They were so tiny you would have needed a microscope to see them. They were a lot like single-celled creatures called bacteria, which are still around today. Like humans, bacteria and their ancestors are organisms that breathe oxygen and prefer temperatures that aren't too hot or too cold. . . aren't they?

OH NO THEY AREN'T!

Early life-forms such as **bacteria** lived on an Earth that looked very different. There was no oxygen, and it was a lot hotter than it is today. Massive storms and volcanic eruptions were frequent.

Just like their ancient ancestors, many bacteria today make their homes in extreme habitats such as freezing glaciers and superheated hot springs—places where most animals and plants would never consider living. I suppose home is where the heart is!

It's a balmy 167 degrees out!

Life on Earth stayed in the sea for billions of years. The first living things to make a home on dry land were early plants and bug-like animals. . . weren't they?

OH NO THEY WEREN'T

The first life-forms to leave the ancient seas were—once again—single-celled organisms like bacteria, as well as plant-like **algae**. Plants were the first living things made up of more than one cell to make it on to land. Plants were followed by the ancestors of modern insects, spiders, millipedes, and other creepy-crawly critters that would, over time, grow to the size of small dogs and have wingspans larger than many modern birds!

ANCIENT SEAS

The ancient seas swarmed with all sorts of fish-like creatures.

Did you know that some of the first fish were built like tanks? Many had armor-like plates on their bodies to protect them from predators. And for good reason! Predators like the formidable **Dunkleosteus** were monsters of the sea, possibly up to 33 feet (10 meters) long.

Still a champion chomper!

Dunkleosteus had razor-sharp teeth that sliced prey into chunks for easier swallowing and, although it lived over 350 million years ago, its jaws are still among the strongest of any animal!

Giant armored fish shared the seas with much-smaller animals such as trilobites. These bug-like creatures looked a bit like modern woodbugs. But because all trilobites became extinct—or died out—about 250 million years ago, they didn't make much of an impact on prehistoric Earth. . . did they?

OH YES THEY DID!

Trilobites lived on Earth for nearly 300 million years. That's nearly 1,000 times longer than our human species, who have only clocked up about 300,000 years so far! During their long time in the ancient seas, trilobites evolved into 20,000 different species, ranging from tiny bean-sized critters to others that were as big as a domestic cat. Many had elaborate spines, movable antennae, and fancy tails.

Trilobites for dinner, again?

You'll have to wait over 250 million years if you want chicken.

Predators like **Anomalocaris** relied on trilobites for food—and larger trilobites were often predators themselves. Trilobites also had important jobs as scavengers. They searched the seafloor for any edible bits that fell from above, including the poop of other animals. *Bon appétit!*

AGE OF REPTILES

About 250 million years ago, after trilobites and armored fish became extinct, it was time for reptiles to reign. The most well known of these prehistoric reptiles are the gigantic dinosaurs. They're the largest animals that have ever lived on Earth. . . aren't they?

OH NO THEY AREN'T!

Some dinosaurs were definitely huge. One of the largest, **Supersaurus**, was between 100–130 feet (30–40 meters) long—about the length of three and a half school buses—and as tall as a four-story building! But even Supersaurus would be dwarfed by the blue whale. **Blue whales** are just as long as Supersaurus, but nearly 28 tons (25 metric tons) heavier!

At the other end of the scale, many dinosaurs were definitely not huge. The smallest found so far was the teeny hummingbird-sized **Oculudentavis**.

actual size

Dinosaurs dominated the Earth for about 200 million years. They were the only predators on land, in the oceans, and in the skies. . . weren't they?

OH NO THEY WEREN'T!

None of the **reptiles** that swam in the seas and flew through the air were actually dinosaurs. In the oceans, there were two main groups of reptiles: **plesiosaurs** and **mosasaurs**. Most plesiosaurs had long necks and streamlined, seal-like bodies. The Loch Ness Monster is said to look like a plesiosaur!

Plesiosaur to meet you!

Mosasaurs had shorter necks and were apex predators—they ate everything, including plesiosaurs and other mosasaurs. Did you know that mosasaurs are related to today's lizards and snakes? The difference is, the ancient giants were nearly as long as a bowling lane.

As for the enormous prehistoric flying reptiles, they were called **pterosaurs**. The largest was Quetzalcoatlus, with a wingspan as wide as a school bus is long. It still holds the record as the largest flying creature ever.

AGE OF MAMMALS

About 66 million years ago, an asteroid from space about as wide as Mount Everest is tall crashed into Earth with the power of 10 million atomic bombs. In the years that followed, over 75 per cent of all plant and animal species disappeared. This included the dinosaurs, which are gone forever. . . aren't they?

OH NO THEY AREN'T!

One group of dinosaurs survived the extinction to become hugely successful, and most of us see them every day—birds. All birds are dinosaurs and closely related to the predatory **Velociraptor**, known for its sharp, sickle-shaped claws. Remember this the next time you have eggs at breakfast. They were laid by a dinosaur!

I should've ordered scrambled eggs!

Some prehistoric birds would grow into massive forms and flourish. But another group would grow even bigger: mammals. Humans are mammals, and so are cats and dogs, cows, horses, pandas, elephants, and dolphins. We mammals all have hair, and we all produce milk to feed to our young. Unlike other animals, all mammals give birth to live young. . . don't they?

OH NO THEY DON'T!

Giving birth to live young is relatively rare—although mammals do it, only some **fish** do, along with a small number of reptiles, **amphibians,** and **insects.** The vast majority of these animals lay eggs instead, and many ancient mammals did too.

Two types of living mammals still lay eggs today: the **platypus** and four species of **echidna**, a mammal that looks a bit like a hedgehog. They all live in Australia or New Guinea.

With the extinction of the non-avian dinosaurs (that is, all of them except the birds), mammals filled many of the dinosaur's niches in each ecosystem. There were giant predators, even larger plant-eaters, mammals that flew, and mammals that returned to the ocean.

Did you know that whales and dolphins evolved from mammals related to modern-day cows and pigs? Seals evolved from otter-like animals, and manatees are related to elephants!

GREEN PLANET
THE AIR WE BREATHE

light energy

oxygen (O_2)

Earth's biomass is the total mass of living material on our planet, and about 80 per cent of it is made up of plants. That's a really big garden—and we should be thankful because plants produce the oxygen we breathe. They also provide food for most living things. Without plants, there would be no chocolate brownies, no strawberries, and no french fries!

Speaking of food, plants don't eat like we do. They're life-forms that get all the food they need from the Sun. . . aren't they?

carbon dioxide (CO_2)

water (H_2O)

OH NO THEY AREN'T!

Plants do use sunlight to make food through a process called **photosynthesis.** But to do this, they also require water, carbon dioxide from the air, and vitamins and minerals from the soil.

vitamins and minerals

Some plants are parasites—they depend on other plants for their food. Parasitic plants can only survive by taking food from another plant, called the host. The **mistletoe** hanging over doorways at Christmas is an example of a parasitic plant. In the wild, mistletoe attaches itself to the branches of other trees and absorbs some water and nutrients from the host tree. It's not quite the kiss you want under the mistletoe!

Don't touch anything!

Some plants have an extra source of nutrition—they eat meat! The **Venus flytrap** is an example of this kind of carnivorous plant. Its leaves look like little tooth-lined jaws and have special trigger hairs that are sensitive to touch. The hairs tell the leaf to close when prey touches them, then the plant's chemicals digest the prey. Venus flytraps generally eat insects and spiders, but other types of carnivorous plants have been known to trap larger prey such as frogs, rats, lizards, and even birds!

LEAFY GIANTS

The blue whale might be larger than any dinosaur, but did you know that the largest land organism ever is a plant? The giant sequoia is a tree from California that makes a blue whale look like a pygmy mouse. They can grow taller than Big Ben or the Statue of Liberty! Their thick trunks make them massively heavy.

400ft

300ft

200ft

100ft

Redwoods might be the tallest land organisms, but the tallest living creatures of all time live in the sea. They're plants called kelp. . . aren't they?

OH NO THEY AREN'T!

Kelp might look like plants, but they're actually organisms called algae, a diverse group that generally photosynthesize and mostly live in water.

Giant kelp form vast underwater forests that shelter all kinds of marine life, including playful sea otters.

Like plants, most algae produce oxygen, but they're not as important because they're only small producers. . . aren't they?

OH NO THEY AREN'T!

Trillions of tiny algae live in the oceans. They're called **phytoplankton**, and they produce most of the oxygen we breathe. This is because the oceans, where phytoplankton live, cover about 70 per cent of Earth's surface—and also because there's a lot of plankton in the ocean. Phytoplankton helps to feed countless fish, crabs, and other marine creatures. Without plankton, the world's oceans would die!

FIVE A DAY

Vegetables and fruits are part of a healthy diet—and they also taste great! Let's make a salad with cucumbers, lettuce, tomatoes, bell peppers, and carrots. These are all delicious vegetables. . . aren't they?

OH NO THEY AREN'T!

Carrots and lettuce are vegetables, but **tomatoes, cucumbers,** and **bell peppers** are fruits. So are **nuts** and **avocados!** Fruits are the parts of a plant that contain seeds. Plants produce fruits to trick animals like birds and squirrels—and humans, too—into spreading their seeds far and wide.

When a deer crunches into an apple, they may go somewhere else to eat it. This lets the apple's seeds hitch a ride to a new location where they can sprout, after traveling through the deer's stomach and exiting out the bottom in its poop.

This fruit salad of cucumbers and bell peppers hits the spot!

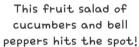

So the next time someone asks for a fruit salad, whip up a bowl of tomatoes and cucumbers alongside the apple slices and berries!

Speaking of berries, what are your favorite berries? Strawberries, blackberries, and raspberries are probably in your top five. They're some of the most popular berries. . . aren't they?

Despite their names, strawberries, blackberries, and raspberries aren't really berries. A **berry** is a type of fruit that forms from a single flower and contains its seeds inside. All of the "berries" above are compound fruits, which means a group of fruits packed tightly together. Also, strawberries have seeds on the outside.

OH NO THEY AREN'T!

But my name is Strawberry. I should be the berry—not the two of you!

Some fruits that really are berries include blueberries, gooseberries, and cranberries. But watermelons, avocados, and bananas are also berries! They are made up of a single fleshy fruit with the seeds inside.

FLOWER POWER

Flowers are the showiest parts of a plant. They're brightly colored and smell really nice. Flowers are just pretty decorations. . . aren't they?

OH NO THEY AREN'T!

Flowers make a dust-like substance called pollen. When **pollen** moves from one flower to another, part of the second flower develops into a fruit. Without flowers, there would be no pollen. Without pollen, there'd be no fruits and no seeds. Also, no fruit salad!

There's more to me than my good looks!

You're also a tasty meal!

Butterflies, bees, and other insects carry pollen from plant to plant, so they are called pollinators. Pollen gets stuck on to their bodies while they drink a sweet liquid called nectar from flowers. When the insects fly away to find more nectar, the pollen hitches a ride and drops off on the new flower. Insects are the only pollinators. . . aren't they?

OH NO THEY AREN'T!

Insects are the main **pollinators,** but many other animals carry pollen too. A number of plants in the tropics depend on hummingbirds. The flowers on these plants are usually tube-shaped—the perfect fit for a hummingbird's long beak.

Bats are the main pollinators of several plants, such as the giant saguaro cactus, whose flowers open in the evening. The mouse-like honey possum from Australia loves nectar. As they feed, their little faces get covered in the pollen of their favorite flowers, banksias.

Did you know that wind is also a pollinator? Grasses, trees, and other plants with small flowers that don't make nectar use the wind to blow their pollen away—sometimes for miles and miles. One of the main triggers for hay fever is when there's a lot of pollen in the air. ACHOO!!!

FUN GUYS

Mushrooms are nature's recyclers. They decompose—or break down—dead plant matter such as logs and fallen leaves to help make soil. Mushrooms sometimes grow in a circle around the base of a dead tree, and some people say these are places where fairies hold dance parties! Mushrooms are strange plants that don't photosynthesize. . . aren't they?

OH NO THEY AREN'T!

Cap-tivating stuff, isn't it?

It's true that mushrooms don't photosynthesize, but that's less surprising when you know that they're not plants. They belong to a group called **fungi**, which also includes the yeasts that we use to make bread, as well as the mold growing in your bathroom.

Did you know that what we call a mushroom is only the visible part of the fungus? The majority of a mushroom's body is hidden underground. Many fungi create networks of fungal filaments called **mycelia**, which they use to absorb nutrients from the soil.

These mycelial networks can grow to enormous sizes. One **honey fungus** from a national park in the Pacific Northwest has a mycelial network about three times the size of Central Park in New York!

24

Unlike animals, fungi don't talk or make any sounds. They're organisms with no way of communicating with each other. . . aren't they?

OH NO THEY **AREN'T!**

Fungi use mycelia to communicate with each other and with plants. Mycelia from individual fungi connect into giant networks that tap into the roots of trees and other plants.

Through these connections, plants and fungi share nutrients. They also send **chemical messages**, warning each other about illnesses, attacks by insects, and changes in the soil. It's like an underground internet that links nearly every plant and fungus in the forest!

An underground network of secret messages!

UNDER THE SEA
SURF AND TURF

Fish rule the seas and waterways. They've evolved into an incredible variety of shapes and sizes to live in almost every watery habitat. They never leave the water because they're only able to breathe in water. . . aren't they?

OH NO THEY AREN'T!

All animals need **oxygen**. Most fish get oxygen from water using organs called gills. But some fish can breathe air like we do! Some catfish species live in muddy pools with very little oxygen. They survive by gulping air. **Lungfish**, as you can guess, have lungs, which are air-breathing organs.

A fish out of water no more!

When their pond dries up, they wait for the next rainstorm while asleep underground—sometimes for over a year!

Did you know some fish can move around on land? Walking **catfish** have special feet-like fins that let them wriggle from one pool of water to another.

Some fish might be able to survive on land, but crabs are creatures that only live in water. . . aren't they?

OH NO THEY AREN'T!

Some crab species only live on land. The melon-sized **coconut crab** lives on islands in the Pacific and Indian Oceans. They hatch in the sea and move to dry land when they grow up. Adult coconut crabs can't swim at all. They will drown in water!

Home is where the bromeliad is!

Did you know that there's a crab that lives inside a plant? The **bromeliad crab** makes its home in bromeliads—tropical plants that grow on the branches of trees. High up in the forest, bromeliads collect rainwater in their leaves, creating a tiny freshwater pond. It makes the perfect home for a crab that has never seen the ocean.

MARINE METROPOLIS

Coral reefs are the megacities of the oceans. Countless creatures make their homes in these underwater oases. It's only possible because of coral. Corals aren't alive, though. They're basically rocks. . . aren't they?

OH NO THEY AREN'T!

Corals are colonies of creatures that live together. They're like apartment complexes where everyone builds their home on and around their neighbors. And we're talking about millions of neighbors! Most individual corals are very small, but together they can make large structures.

Some groups form flat structures shaped like dinner plates. Others branch out like the antlers of an elk. And some have different shapes, like the **brain corals** that are shaped like, well. . . brains! The **Great Barrier Reef** in Australia is so large it can be seen from space!

Groups of different corals growing next to each other form reefs.

Did you know that many sea creatures, from fish to shrimp and octopuses, use coral reefs as nurseries? They lay their eggs in coral reefs, where they're protected from the currents of the open sea.

Corals are only found in the tropics. . . aren't they?

OH NO THEY AREN'T!

Species of corals can be found in all but the coldest waters. The brightly colored **red coral** is found in the Mediterranean Sea. There are deep-water corals living in underwater canyons near Canada, Antarctica, and Scandinavia, where temperatures approach freezing!

Did you know that some corals live a very long time? There are coral colonies that are over 4,000 years old, making corals some of the oldest living creatures on our planet!

OCEANIC ORCHESTRA

Life in the sea must be very peaceful.
Sea creatures are silent. . . aren't they?

OH NO THEY AREN'T!

Creatures like octopuses and jellyfish are silent, but there are still many sounds beneath the waves. Many whales, including the enormous **sperm whale**, use echolocation to navigate and find prey. They make clicking noises, which travel through the water. When the sound waves hit an object and bounce back, the whale can tell how far away a fish or an underwater mountain is—and also what kind of mountain or fish it is. A sperm whale's clicks are nearly as loud as a jet engine. They travel for miles in the open ocean!

It's not just whales that are noisy. Many species of **toadfish**, including some called midshipmen, make droning sounds like a foghorn. **Herring** make ticking noises by pushing bubbles out of their bottoms! With squealing rays, crunching sea urchins, hooting batfish, snapping shrimps, drumming drum fish, and singing whales, the ocean is a symphony.

There might be plenty of sounds in the water, but there aren't any smells. . . are there?

OH YES THERE ARE!

Undersea predators follow smells and other chemical trails to find their prey. Many creatures release special scents called **pheromones**, which are used to attract mates and mark the boundaries of their territories or homes.

Did you know that fish have more senses than we do? Aside from touch, taste, smell, sight, and hearing, some fish can sense **electricity**, **pressure**, and **magnetism**. Deep-sea fish and mantis shrimps also have superhero vision. They can see colors that are invisible to humans.

SWIMMING THE SEVEN SEAS

The world's oceans cover about 70 per cent of Earth's surface, creating many different habitats. Cold-water loving whales spend their time in cooler habitats. Tropical swimmers like sea turtles stay in habitats where it's warm. . . don't they?

Animals like sea turtles and whales **migrate**, taking long journeys across different ocean habitats to find food or raise their young. **Gray whales** have one of the longest migrations.

OH NO THEY DON'T!

In summertime, they feed in cold Arctic waters by turning on their side and scooping up bottom-sediment. They use their comb-like baleen to strain ghost shrimp and amphipod crustaceans from the sediments. When fall comes, they navigate to the warm waters of the Gulf of California—a safe place to raise baby whales.

The gold-medal winner is the **Arctic tern**, a bird that spends much of its life living over the ocean, in the air. Their migrations span the globe, from the Arctic to the Antarctic. It's a lifetime of voyaging that in total would make the equivalent of three trips to the Moon and back! The **leatherback sea turtle** is another champion migrator. These marine reptiles cover thousands of miles every year, crossing entire oceans!

Did you know that some sea creatures migrate up and down in the water instead of across it? This is called vertical migration. **Humboldt squid** spend the daytime deep below the surface, where they hide from predators.

Once the Sun sets, they migrate up to feed near the surface. Predators like tuna, which love eating squid, follow their favorite food up to the surface for a midnight snack.

CREEPY-CRAWLIES
WORLD WIDE WEB

Some of the smallest animals are creepy-crawly insects. Did you know that nearly 80 per cent of all animal species are insects? That's a lot of ants and bees and butterflies—and lots of spiders, too! Spiders are insects. . . aren't they?

OH NO THEY AREN'T!

Spiders are **arachnids**. They're related to insects, but while insects have six legs, most arachnids have eight. **Scorpions** are also arachnids. **Ticks** are too, although they're born with six legs and grow two more as adults. Daddy longlegs is the name we give to a number of different arachnids with tiny bodies and very long legs.

Looking great with legs of eight!

Spiders use spider silk to spin webs. They're all skilled web-spinners. . . aren't they?

OH NO THEY AREN'T!

Plenty of spiders spin webs, but many species can't—they have other ways of getting food. For example, **wolf spiders** are excellent hunters. Some chase down their prey like wolves! The females use spider silk to make sticky pouches for their eggs, which they carry on their bodies while hunting. Brightly colored **crab spiders** make silk drop lines for safety. If the spiders are dislodged whilst catching insects to eat, they can haul themselves back up again. Female crab spiders can also change color to blend in with their surroundings. It helps them hide so they can ambush their lunch.

A nub a day keeps the doctor away!

Did you know that there's a vegetarian spider? The thorn trees of Central America grow little packets of protein on the tips of their leaves. One type of **jumping spider** lives in these thorn trees and eats the nutritious nubs. The spiders are very small, with shiny green stripes on their bodies. They will occasionally eat an ant larva or two, but thorn tree protein and nectar are their favorite foods.

SOCIAL BUTTERFLIES

What's the difference between a moth and a butterfly? Butterfly wings close when they land, while a resting moth's wings stay flat. Butterfly antennae are slender and clubbed, while moth antennae can look more like feathers. All butterflies are active during the day, and all moths are active at night. . . aren't they?

Flat and fabulous!

OH NO THEY AREN'T!

Nectar nosh!

Butterflies are daytime animals and most moths are nocturnal, which means they are active at night. But some moth species love the daytime. The **hummingbird hawk-moth** is one that is most active when the Sun is up. These moths hover like hummingbirds to sip nectar. The **striped Jersey tiger moth**, found in southern England, is also diurnal, or active during the day.

Come here often?

Did you know that the **monarch butterfly** has one of the longest migrations of any insect? They spend the winter in Mexico and California and spend summers in forests across North America. Millions of monarchs turn the trees in California and Mexico orange as they rest in enormous social gatherings during migrations. Because monarchs don't live very long, it takes many generations for them to complete the round-trip journey.

Another difference between butterflies and moths is that moths are dull compared to butterflies. They're all brown and gray. . . aren't they?

OH NO THEY AREN'T!

Many moths are as brightly colored as any butterfly. The **burnet moth** has bright red spots on brilliant blue or black wings.

The **rosy maple moth** is also vibrant. It's fuzzy like a teddy bear with a yellow body, bright pink legs, and pink-and-yellow-striped wings. With their trendy, color-coordinated look, rosy maple moths belong in a fashion show.

SLIME TIME

Slugs and snails are creepy-crawlies that emerge from their hiding places at night and after the rain. Snails carry shells on their backs. Slugs don't. They might be everywhere, but slugs and snails aren't very important. They're just slimy pests. . . aren't they?

OH NO THEY AREN'T!

Slugs and snails are very important to their ecosystem—the community of living things in a particular area. These slimy sliders eat dead and decaying plants, enriching the soil when they poop out their food.

Snails and slugs are also the favorite food for many animals, particularly birds, toads, foxes, and turtles. Metallic-green ground beetles also love a sluggy, snail-y snack.

Did you know that some slugs and snails eat each other? Their fearsome names are a bit of a giveaway: rosy wolf snail, leopard slug, killer snail, and ghost slug.

The world's largest snail is the giant African land snail, whose brown shell is the size of an avocado. The longest slug is the ash black slug, which is about the length of a letter-sized envelope. No matter what size they are, snails and slugs aren't colorful. They're all brown and black. . . aren't they?

OH NO THEY AREN'T!

The **banana slug** is bright yellow. **Candy cane snails** have shells striped with yellows, reds, and purples.

Did you know that the snails and slugs in your yard are related to snails in the ocean? Unlike marine snails, they breathe air with lungs and can't survive underwater. They also can't survive if they dry out. This is why land snails and slugs produce slime—it keeps them moist. Slime also helps them slide along the ground. Without slime, these creepy-crawlies would move even more slowly!

Keep calm and slime on. . .

PULLING YOUR LEG

Insects have six legs. Arachnids have eight. Millipedes are creepy-crawlies with thousands of legs. . . aren't they?

OH NO THEY AREN'T!

Although the word millipede means "a thousand legs," only one species of millipede has over 1,000 legs and the rest have hundreds of legs. Maybe the word "**centipede**" is more accurate. It means "one hundred legs" and, though many types of centipedes have a few hundred legs, some have only thirty. Should we call them thirtypedes?

Who needs legs, anyway?

Earthworms have no legs! They move through the soil by contracting their bodies like an accordion. They also make slime, just like snails and slugs, to make it easier to worm their way around.

Earthworms are cool because if you cut one in half, both pieces will grow into a new worm. . . won't they?

OH NO THEY WON'T!

Time for a new tail.

Did you know that many kinds of animals can grow back arms and legs if a predator bites them off? Some lizards, such as **geckos**, can grow back their tails.

If an earthworm escapes being eaten and is cut in two, only the end with the head will survive. It will grow another tail. As for the other end. . . well, its worming days are over. But earthworms aren't alone in having this animal superpower.

I'm totally claw-some!

Male **fiddler crabs** have one claw that's a lot larger than the other. It's used for fighting and communicating. Many fiddler crabs can grow back this giant claw if it's lost.

Amphibians are animals that spend their childhood in the water and come on land as adults, and several types can grow back their tails as well as their legs. An **axolotl** can even regrow parts of its own heart!

No heartbreak for me!

Fiddle dee dee!

PREDATOR AND PREY
CATCH ME IF YOU CAN

All animals have to eat. Those that eat other animals are called predators. The animals that become their food are called prey. Prey animals like antelope have to be fast to avoid being caught by predators. If animals have managed to survive this long, that must be because they're the fastest animals out there. . . aren't they?

OH NO THEY AREN'T!

The fastest land animal is a predator: the **cheetah**. Cheetahs have been clocked at over 60 miles (100 kilometers) an hour! Luckily for the agile **antelope**, these quick cats can only run at this speed for less than a minute. Antelope aren't quite as fast, but they can run at top speed for longer—so they escape once the cheetah gets tired out.

Being fast isn't the only way to avoid being eaten. There's also safety in numbers. A group has more eyes to watch for predators.

Did you know that many prey animals form herds as protection? Zebras, horses, and buffalo are some examples. Elephants form herds to protect their young, and so did some species of extinct plant-eating dinosaurs, including duck-billed dinosaurs and horned dinosaurs.

Don't even think about it!

Living in herds is common in land animals. But animals that live in water are loners that don't create herds. . . aren't they?

OH NO THEY AREN'T!

Fish form enormous groups called shoals. The largest herring **shoals** include millions of fish! They do this because herring are one of every marine predator's favorite comfort foods! They're eaten by a wide range of animals, from seals and bald eagles to marlin—predatory fish with spear-like bills that are among the fastest swimmers on the planet.

Cute rodents called lemmings form herds when migrating. Herds of lemmings are known to jump off cliffs. . . aren't they?

OH NO THEY AREN'T!

Despite stories of lemming herds jumping off cliffs, they don't do this. The theory spread widely after a popular film staged a fake cliff jump!

DON'T JUMP!

SHARK ATTACK

Sharks are one of the top predators of the seas, and the great white shark is the master of them all! These sharks have jaws so strong they can easily bite through bone. All sharks are fearsome predators. . . aren't they?

OH NO THEY AREN'T!

The largest shark in the world, the **whale shark**, is a gentle giant. Whale sharks eat microscopic plankton and small animals like krill, fish, and squid—but they don't really hunt. These massive sharks swim through the water with their mouths open, eating anything that passes into their stomachs through filters on the inside of their gill slits.

Swim away!
Swim away!

All sharks are very big. . . aren't they?

OH NO THEY'RE NOT!

Uh, oh!

Dwarf lanternsharks, part of the dogfish family of sharks, are the smallest shark species in the world. They're about the size of a cell phone and live deep in the ocean, feeding on shrimp and other deep-sea creatures.

Even though some sharks are small, they're still sharks. And all sharks are apex predators, taking the top spot in the food chain. . . aren't they?

Many sharks are prey for other animals. Seals and sea lions hunt small shark species. Larger sharks also feed on smaller sharks. And young sharks, called pups, are eaten by a wide variety of animals, from fish to birds.

OH NO THEY AREN'T!

Dinner time!

Did you know that even the great white shark is hunted by another animal? **Orcas!** Orcas are highly intelligent dolphins. They form close family groups called pods and work together to hunt prey like great white sharks, seals, other dolphin species, and even much larger whales.

45

HIDE AND SEEK

If prey animals can't outrun a predator, and don't have a herd to offer safety in numbers, they're lunch. . . aren't they?

OH NO THEY AREN'T!

Now you see me, now you don't!

Where did you go?

Many prey species are masters of disguise. **Chameleons** are lizards whose markings often make them look like leaves or branches. They can make small changes to their coloring to better match their surroundings, like becoming darker to match a shadier hiding spot. It's almost like an invisibility cloak!

Blending in with your surroundings, or disguising yourself to look like something else, is called camouflage.

Did you know that the brown coloring of many birds is also a form of camouflage? Brown birds sitting in trees are almost invisible because they match the brown of branches. Speckled birds are also very well camouflaged. The bright specks look like light shining through leaves, the darker patches like shadows. This is why so many baby animals are speckly and brown. Lion cubs and fawns hide in patches of grass or bushes, camouflaged from predators by their coloring.

Hiding in plain sight!

Prey animals are the only ones that use camouflage. . . aren't they?

OH NO THEY AREN'T!

Predators use camouflage to sneak up on prey. One of the most impressive masters of disguise is a marine predator, the **octopus**. Like chameleons, octopuses can change their color. But they have one more trick: they can transform the texture of their bodies! A smooth-bodied octopus will suddenly grow spiky bumps and horns to look like coral or seaweed, while they patiently wait for dinner to swim by.

The stripes on hunters like tigers are also a form of camouflage. They make the big cats difficult to see when stalking prey in forests or tall grass.

WARNING!
GROSS CONTENT ON NEXT PAGE!

47

SMELL YOU LATER

Even the best camouflaged prey might be found by a predator. If they are, they have no other tricks up their sleeve. Now they're definitely lunch. . . aren't they?

OH NO THEY AREN'T!

Yuck!

Take a whiff of this!

Many animals have evolved very effective defenses. **Skunks** have special glands by their tails that squirt a liquid that smells like rotting eggs. Not many hunters will ever chase a skunk again after being sprayed in the face. Yuck!

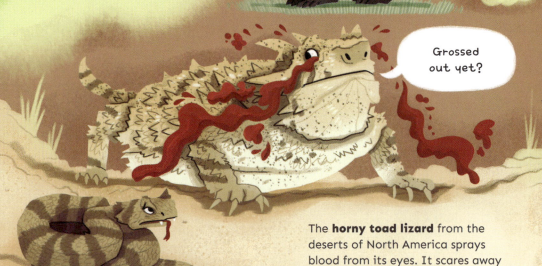

Grossed out yet?

The **horny toad lizard** from the deserts of North America sprays blood from its eyes. It scares away predators by grossing them out!

Maybe the grossest of them all is the **sea cucumber**, a soft-bodied sea creature related to sea stars. When threatened, sea cucumbers vomit out their insides! The internal organs then release a sticky, poisonous chemical that no one wants to eat.

Did you know that predatory animals also use smells? But rather than stinky smells, they use scents that are irresistible. The **orchid mantis** is an insect that looks like the orchid flowers it lives on. Juvenile mantises release chemicals called pheromones that bees, butterflies, and other nectar-loving insects can't resist. The prey that's lured in by the lovely scent makes a nice meal for the mantis. The meat-eating **Venus flytrap** also releases a sweet smell. Insects follow the smell, thinking they'll find nectar. But it's a deadly trap!

Something smells deadly good!

HIGH FLIERS
GOING WITH THE FLOW

Countless living creatures have taken to life in the air. Fish and other aquatic animals don't do this, though. They're unable to leave the water to become airborne. . . aren't they?

OH NO THEY AREN'T!

Flying fish launch themselves out of the water to glide on long wing-like fins. Gliding means soaring in the air for long distances, rather than flapping wings to actively fly. Flying fish leap out of the water, sometimes gliding more than 600 feet (about 200 meters) to escape predators. That's the length of two football fields!

The freshwater versions of **butterflyfish** and **hatchetfish** can also launch themselves into the air. They don't make good pets because they often leap out of fish tanks.

Did you know that there's even a species of gliding squid? **Japanese flying squid** shoot out a powerful jet of water to become airborne, then flap their fins to glide—often in large groups, called shoals.

In fact, lots of animals glide. **Flying squirrels** have wing-like flaps of skin stretched between their wrists and ankles. These flaps act like parachutes when the rodents jump between trees.

Rush-hour traffic. . .

Gliding frogs have similar parachute-like wings—one on each foot. There are also **gliding lizards** and **lemurs,** as well as a group of pouched animals from Australia called **gliders**. These Australian gliders have skin "parachutes" like flying squirrels and leap from flower to flower looking for nectar and pollen.

Did you know that there were even dinosaur gliders? The **scansoriopterygids,** whose long name means "climbing wing," were hawk-sized dinosaurs. They lived in trees and had parachute-like flaps on their arms. These dinosaurs' gliding skills would've helped them jump far to find food and escape predators.

51

HIGH ROLLING

Many animals glide for long distances, but they can only stay up for a limited time. Animals that can truly fly have a big advantage. . . wings! By flapping their wings, fliers can propel themselves through the air. Unlike gliders, fliers can change direction and turn around. Many of these fliers can also glide to save energy, staying aloft for hours or even days. But all flying animals have to return to the ground to sleep. . . don't they?

²z z z

OH NO THEY DON'T!

The **frigate bird** can sleep while flying! They take little naps when soaring on currents.

Sleep-flying again. . .

The **albatross** is one of the most accomplished fliers. They have wingspans as wide as the tallest people and spend most of their lives airborne.

Grounded? Not me!

Did you know that albatrosses can go for years without touching the ground? They often fly for days without stopping, landing on water to catch food and rest, only returning to land to mate.

Birds might fly very far, but they don't fly too high. They're only found close to the surface where there's food. . . aren't they?

OH NO THEY AREN'T!

The **bar-headed goose** lives near alpine lakes—bodies of water high up in the mountains. There's a lot less oxygen at this altitude, so these birds have extra-large lungs and special blood cells to hold more oxygen. Mountain climbers have spotted these birds flying over Mount Everest!

Even more impressive is the **Rüppell's griffon vulture**. These birds follow high passes through the mountains, flying up to altitudes of 4.5 miles (7.3 kilometers), with some even reaching as high as the peak of Mount Everest!

The Himalayas, crossed off my bucket list.

AERIAL ACROBATICS

Flying animals are impressive, but they can't match the agility of machine-made airplanes and helicopters. Animals are only good at flying in straight lines. . . aren't they?

OH NO THEY AREN'T!

Dragonflies and other insects are incredible aerial acrobats. They can hover and make sudden twists and turns that even a drone can't manage. Dragonflies are one of the fastest insect fliers, clocking speeds of up to 15 miles (25 kilometers) per hour!

Hummingbirds are also incredible fliers. Like insects, they can fly backwards!

Did you know that the world's smallest bird is a hummingbird? The tiny **bee hummingbird** is the size of a paperclip! It takes a lot of energy to fuel the acrobatics of hummingbirds. Their favorite food is nectar, and they tend to eat every ten minutes when they're awake. Talk about a sugar rush!

Bats are the only mammals that fly. They're mostly nocturnal, which means their eyes are equipped with special night vision. . . aren't they?

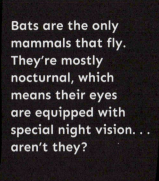

OH NO THEY AREN'T!

Most bats are active at night, and they don't use their eyes to hunt. Like dolphins, many bats use **echolocation** instead of their eyes! While airborne, they make high-pitched clicks that bounce off trees and rocks—and prey animals—to create a sound-picture of their surroundings. With their awesome echolocation and flying skills, these bats can catch and eat prey in mid-air!

Sure is a quiet night. . .

Flying insects make up the bulk of their prey, but did you know that there are **fish-eating bats?**

These clever creatures fly inches above the water, using echolocation to scan for splashes made by fish. When the right type of splash is spotted, the bats lower their clawed hind-legs to snatch dinner from the water. Mid-air seafood!

GROUNDED

All birds are fliers. . . aren't they?

OH NO THEY AREN'T!

As they've evolved, many bird species have lost the ability to fly. **Ostriches** are one example. They're the largest living birds, but their bodies are too heavy to leave the ground, and their wings aren't the right shape for flying.

Ostriches are built for running, and they can run really fast. They use their big wings for balance, communication, and as a defense against predators.

Tall, dark, and handsome— that's us!

Did you know that until the 1400s, New Zealand was home to nine species of flightless birds called moas? Some were even taller than ostriches! The **moas** were prey for the world's largest eagle, the now-extinct Haast's eagle, which attacked smaller moas from above. Although moas were big, there was another bird that was even larger. The biggest, bulkiest flightless bird that ever lived was the **elephant bird** of Madagascar. Sadly, both moas and elephant birds are now gone, likely hunted to extinction by humans.

Another extinct flightless bird is the dodo. Dodos all died out about 400 years ago. This is because they were slow and simple-minded. . . weren't they?

OH NO THEY WEREN'T!

The **dodo** was a flightless pigeon, about the size of a turkey—making it the biggest pigeon species ever. Dodos had no natural predators on their island home. When humans arrived, the birds had no natural fear of them and were easy prey.

This pigeon sure knows how to dodo it big!

Hunting, habitat destruction, and the introduction of rats and cats to their island home drove them to extinction. They're just another in the list of flightless island birds that became extinct because of humans.

Don't call me an owl!

Did you know that there's a species of flightless parrot? The endangered **kākāpō** is a green-and-yellow parrot from New Zealand. They have owl-like faces—and, like owls, they're nocturnal. Luckily for these flightless birds, they're protected. Conservation efforts are helping to keep them healthy and happy as they waddle around on the ground.

GEOLOGICAL TIMELINE

The geologic timeline is a chart that shows the story of our planet from when it first formed about 4.5 billion years ago.

This timeline also shows the evolution of life on Earth, from the first single-celled organisms to plants, insects, dinosaurs, and us! The timeline is divided into eons that stretch for billions of years, then shorter eras and periods.

Today we are in the **Phanerozoic Eon**, the **Cenozoic Era**, and the **Quaternary Period**.

Right before 4 a.m., single-celled life appears, then algae a little after 2 p.m.

At 5 p.m. we see the first multicellular organisms, but it's only after 8 p.m. that the oceans fill with aquatic creatures.

Imagine that all of Earth's long history was squeezed into a 24-hour day, with the planet formed at midnight.

At the last few seconds before midnight, humans appear—fashionably late, as always!

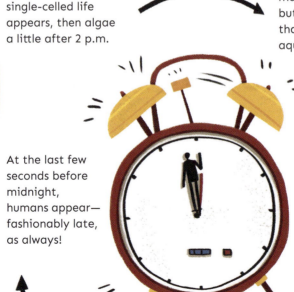

Plants start to grow on dry land at 9:30 p.m., and half an hour later, animals join them.

Dinosaurs dominate for an hour, from about 10:40 p.m. to 11:40 p.m., before mammals and birds take over.

CENOZOIC
66 MYA–TODAY

QUATERNARY
2.5 MYA–TODAY

NEOGENE
23 MYA–2.5 MYA

PALEOGENE
66 MYA–23 MYA

MESOZOIC
252 MYA–66 MYA

CRETACEOUS
145 MYA–66 MYA

JURASSIC
201 MYA–145 MYA

TRIASSIC
252 MYA–201 MYA

PALEOZOIC
541 MYA–252 MYA

PERMIAN
299 MYA–252 MYA

CARBONIFEROUS
359 MYA–299 MYA

DEVONIAN
419 MYA–359 MYA

SILURIAN
444 MYA–419 MYA

ORDOVICIAN
485 MYA–444 MYA

CAMBRIAN
539 MYA–485 MYA

PHANEROZOIC
541 MYA–TODAY

PROTEROZOIC
2.5 BYA–541 MYA

ARCHEAN
4.0 BYA–2.5 BYA

HADEAN
4.6 BYA–4.0 BYA

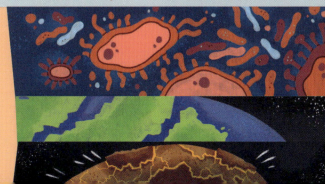

GLOSSARY

aerodynamic shaped to move easily through the air or water, often with a smooth, torpedo-like shape.

algae a group of simple organisms, including seaweeds, that usually photosynthesize and live in water.

alpine occurring in high, mountainous regions where there's often snow or ice on the ground in the winter.

amphibian any vertebrate animal, such as a frog, that begins life living in water but then changes body shape and lives on land as an adult.

apex predator a meat-eating organism at the top of its food chain, which is not eaten by any other animal.

arachnid one of a group of invertebrate animals with eight legs, such as a spider or scorpion.

bacteria tiny single-celled organisms that can usually only be seen with a microscope, and which were some of the very first life-forms on Earth.

biomass the total mass of living material on the planet.

bromeliad a type of plant that often lives in rain forests, deserts, or mountains.

camouflage a way that plants and animals can protect themselves by blending in with their surroundings, making them very difficult to see.

cells the basic building blocks of all living things.

colony a group of organisms living closely together that depend on one another for food and protection.

coral reef an underwater structure made from coral colonies living closely together; reefs are marine habitats that support a great diversity of life.

decompose to rot and break down into simpler materials that can be used again.

diurnal most active during the daytime.

echolocation the use of high-pitched sounds to find your way in the dark, or low visibility, by hearing their echoes bounce back.

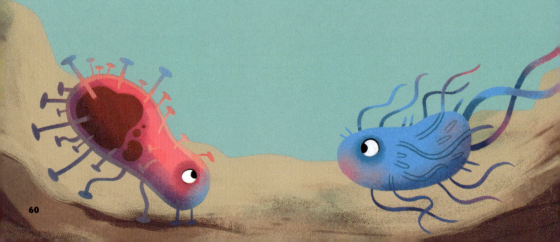

ecosystem a habitat and the community of living things living there, which all interact with each other.

endangered at risk of becoming extinct.

evolution the natural process by which living creatures change over long periods of time, as some species die out and others develop into new forms.

extinct having completely died out as a species, so that no more are left.

food chain a visual way of showing how the Sun's energy is passed on through living creatures; it often begins with a plant getting energy from the Sun and then follows the energy as different animals eat the plant and then each other.

fungus (plural **fungi**) a type of living organism that feeds by decomposing other organisms.

gills organs used by fish and other aquatic creatures to breathe underwater.

glide to move gradually down through the air to the ground, using flaps or wings to control the flight.

habitat the place where an organism lives; ponds and forests are both types of habitat.

herd a group of animals from the same species that live together for protection; deer, antelope, and wild horses live in herds.

invertebrate an animal that does not have a spine (backbone).

lungs organs that allow animals to breathe air.

mammal a vertebrate that has hair or fur and makes milk to feed its young.

marine relating to or living in the ocean.

migration the seasonal movement of animals to find food and avoid the harsh conditions of winter.

multicellular made up of many cells; plants and animals are multicellular.

mycelium the network of tiny, thread-like structures made by fungi that help them grow, gather nutrients, and communicate.

nocturnal most active at night.

nutrients the substances that organisms need to survive and grow; animals get nutrients from the food they eat.

organism any living thing, from microscopic bacteria to gigantic whales.

oxygen a gas in the air that all animals need to survive.

parasite an organism that lives on or inside another and causes harm to its host.

pheromones chemical signals produced by living organisms to communicate with each other.

photosynthesis the process that plants and algae use to convert sunlight into the chemical energy that they need to survive and grow.

plankton very small creatures that float in aquatic and marine ecosystems and form the bottom rung of many aquatic food chains.

pollen a powder produced by plants, which they use to make seeds.

pollinator an animal that carries pollen from one plant to another, usually unintentionally.

predator a living thing that hunts and eats other animals.

prey an organism that is hunted for food.

pterosaur an extinct flying reptile with leathery wings that lived millions of years ago.

regenerate to grow back a body part.

reptile one of a group of vertebrate animals, including snakes and dinosaurs, that are generally scaly and lay eggs.

scavenger an animal that finds dead animals to eat instead of hunting live ones.

seed the part of a plant that can grow into a brand-new plant.

shoal a group of fish or squid that live together.

single-celled made up of only one cell; some types of bacteria are single-celled organisms.

species a group of organisms that all have the same characteristics and are able to reproduce together.

tropics the areas close to the Equator, which form a warm habitat where it rains a lot.

vertebrate an animal with a spine (backbone).

yeast a type of single-celled fungus; some yeasts are used to make bread and other foods.

ABOUT THE AUTHOR

Eric Huang was born in New Jersey and grew up in California. He loved mythology, nature, comic books, and, more than anything else. . . dinosaurs. When Eric went to college he studied paleontology, hoping to find fossils. But life took him all the way to Australia, where he found kangaroos and koalas instead. Since then, Eric has worked with Disney, Penguin Books, and LEGO—and found a few fossils along the way. He now teaches at City, University of London, writes books, and makes podcasts.

Acknowledgments

Thank you to Holly, Alice, and Nancy for all of your invaluable feedback. Thank you Shannon for signing up this series. And thanks to Angela, Brian, Elias, Emma, Lynsey, Nic, and my mom for pushing me to write!
Eric Huang

ABOUT THE ILLUSTRATOR

Sam Caldwell is an illustrator based in Glasgow where he lives with his wife and two cats: Tonks and Luna. Sam loves inventing characters and creating images packed full of detail, texture, and color. He is passionate about animals and nature, and when he's not drawing, Sam can often be found exploring the Scottish Highlands. He has illustrated many books for children, including the award-winning *Do Bears Poop in the Woods*?

Acknowledgments

A big thanks to Kat and Susi for all of the fantastic design work and steering of the ship on this series. Thank you also Doreen, Kate, and Tom for the opportunity and continued support.

Sam Caldwell